The Virtue of Virtues

A CCD TEXTBOOK

Linda Hourihan

iUniverse®

THE VIRTUE OF VIRTUES

iUniverse books may be ordered through booksellers or by contacting:

iUniverse
1663 Liberty Drive
Bloomington, IN 47403
www.iuniverse.com
1-800-Authors (1-800-288-4677)

ISBN: 978-1-5320-9461-3 (sc)
ISBN: 978-1-5320-9462-0 (e)

Print information available on the last page.

iUniverse rev. date: 01/31/2020

Contents

APPENDIX – TEACHER AND PARENT OBJECTIVES

DEDICATION

I dedicate this book to the Holy Trinity: God my loving Father, Jesus His Son and my Savior, and the virtue-filled Holy Spirit without whose inspiration and spiritual guidance this work would not have been possible.

Special thanks also go to my husband, John Hourihan, who encouraged me to publish this book for the First Printing in 1999. I taught this book in the Worcester Diocese as part of the sixth-grade CCD curriculum. John continues to encourage me to have this book rereleased for a Second Printing in 2020.

I wish to thank all the teachers and parents who taught this program in the past, though short in length of lessons, is long in life saving virtues for our youth which they can use for the rest of their lives. These virtues, first taught by Jesus Christ to all the faithful, are the same, then as now, and continue to be a tremendous help as the moral compass for our youth, teachers and parents, through the strong undercurrents of challenges to virtue based morality today.

FOREWORD

The Virtue of Virtues is a sixth grade, virtue-based morality curriculum designed to be incorporated into existing CCD parish programs. The seven lessons may be taught once each month during the CCD year or in a seven-week block from October to December at the start of the CCD year. Both methods have proven to be successful.

Parents can use this organized approach to teach virtues to their children, since *The Virtue of Virtues* may be taught one hour each night for one week, once a week for seven weeks, or one a month for seven months, as the parish programs have been taught. Parents can teach their children individually or in a comfortable setting with other parents and their children.

I. Theological Virtues

A. Faith
B. Hope
C. Love

Hi. My name is Linda. My assignment is to investigate half-truths and correct them. Did you know that if something is a half-truth, it's really a lie? There are some mixed-up messages I'm hearing about morality. Some people don't know God and think they can live life without Him. They only know half of the truth about morality and decision making. I just discovered that practicing the virtues God gives us is the answer. I'm on a virtues hunt, and I need your help. I've got my notebook out. The questions I need to answer about virtues are: what, why, how, when, who and where are they? Get your nose for news ready.

Fact number one is: Virtues mean good habits. The more we do something, the more it becomes a habit for us. We get into doing good habits or bad habits. When we practice good habits that lead us closer to God, we are practicing virtues.

Fact number two is: The word *theological* means "having to do with God." The theological virtues are faith, hope and love. These virtues are given to us by God. We get stronger in faith, hope and love the more we practice them.

Dictionary

Theological Virtues: Faith, Hope, Love

Virtue: Moral excellence, uprightness, goodness

Faith: Active belief in God, confidence, trust

Hope: Desire or expectation in God's promises

Love: Strong and tender affection, deep devotion, God

My Notes

_____

_____

_____

_____

_____

What?

A FAMILY VISIT

"Uncle Ed is coming for a visit from Arizona next week," Dad announced at dinner one night. Everyone at the table cheered to have their favorite relative in their home again.

Ben and Jill loved to spend time with Uncle Ed because he would always tell them funny stories and take them fishing. The last time Uncle Ed visited, Jill caught the biggest fish, but couldn't get it off the hook. Ben caught the most fish, and Uncle Ed caught an old sock.

Mom's eyes lit up too, but then she asked, "What if he can't get the time off from work? He just got that new job!"

"We will just hope for the best," Dad said. "We will have to have faith in him to do what he can."

As the time grew closer for Uncle Ed to arrive, Mom, Dad, Ben and Jill waited with longing hearts. They were hoping things would work out with his job so that he could still visit. They had faith he'd try his best to visit them. And no matter what, Uncle Ed knew the family loved him very much.

Why?

Why was this visit important?

_____

_____

What virtues did the family have to have while waiting?

_____

_____

How can we better live the virtues of faith, hope and love in our lives?

_____

_____

How?

Write a time when you needed to practice faith, hope and love on the lines below.

_____

_____

When?

THE GREAT FLOOD

Years after God created all the world and the people in it, people began to live without virtues. Instead, they started to live only for themselves. They became a greedy, selfish and sinful people. They lived their lives as if God did not exist. God was sorry he had ever created people, except for Noah and his family.

God said to Noah, "I will destroy all living things on earth. Because of them, the earth is filled with evil and violence. As for you and your family, make an ark out of cypress wood. I shall destroy every living thing. But with you, I will make a promise. This promise shall be called a covenant."

Then God commanded, "Take two of every living creature upon the earth and bring them into the ark to keep them alive with you. Also, take some of every kind of food that is eaten for you and the creatures."

As soon as Noah had finished this task, the rains came and flooded the earth for forty days and nights. Noah was scared during the devastating storm that rocked the ark, but he still practiced the virtues of faith, hope and love. God remembered Noah and the covenant He had made with him.

At the end of the forty days, Noah sent out a raven from the ark to find dry land. But the raven returned. After seven more days, Noah sent out a dove, which returned with an olive leaf. Another seven days later, when Noah sent out the dove, it did not return. Noah knew God had kept His promise.

Who?

The virtues of faith, hope and love are called theological virtues. It is God who gives us these virtues. We become stronger in faith, hope and love the more we use them. It is also true that the less we practice faith, hope and love, the weaker those virtues become in us.

God has given each of us the gifts of faith, hope and love so that we can have faith in Him, hope in Him and love Him. But God has also placed His faith in us, His hope in us, and His love in us. How are we responding?

When Saint Pope John Paul II spoke to youth on March 11, 1979, he told them, "Jesus loves you! Jesus came to this earth to reveal to us and to guarantee to us God's love. He came to love us and to be loved. Let yourselves be loved by Christ!"

Where?

God gave us the virtues of faith, hope and love because he cares for us and wants what is best for us. We are created by God and will someday live with God in heaven. The virtues of faith, hope and love are tools to help us live the way God wants us to live on earth and in heaven.

Examples of situations where I can practice these virtues:

_____

_____

_____

_____

_____

Alternate activities

1. Divide the class into two groups. Group One are the Christians with faith, hope and love. Group Two are the atheists who debate them on their beliefs.
2. Class discussion on what most of the media say to have faith, hope and love in. Discuss TV, magazines, radio, movies and the messages they promote.
3. Brainstorm ideas where the students plan activities, get-togethers, community projects, school projects, or home activities that foster faith, hope and love.

4. Discuss current popular singing artists, movies, et cetera, that demonstrate wholesome entertainment and good moral values.
5. Discuss optional responses to negative messages, other choices they have in each moment, for instance, calling a friend, picking up a good book or a baseball or a basketball.
6. Create a poster about faith, hope and love.

II. Cardinal Virtues

A. Prudence
B. Justice
C. Fortitude
D. Temperance

I need your help to uncover the facts about cardinal virtues. I remembered that the theological virtues of faith, hope and love are given to us by God. Did you know that practicing the cardinal virtues, which are prudence, justice, fortitude, and temperance, help us better live out the theological virtues? Here's the secret: It's just like building blocks. We need to build a strong foundation to live a healthy and moral life.

Fact number one is: Cardinal virtues are the paths on earth that lead to happiness in heaven forever. God created us to live with Him, and for Him, both here on earth and in heaven. It will be very hard to love and serve God on earth and in heaven if we do not walk along this path.

Fact number two is: Just like the theological virtues, the more we practice prudence, justice, fortitude and temperance, the stronger they become in us.

Dictionary

Cardinal virtues: Prudence, temperance, fortitude, justice

Prudence: Wisdom, carefulness, thoughtfulness

Temperance: Moderation, self-control, orderliness

Fortitude: Inner strength, courage, strong character

Justice: Fairness, righteousness, reward of our actions

_____

_____

_____

_____

_____

What?

THE CANDY BAR KID

Julie babysat for the Smith's three-year old daughter last Saturday morning with no problem while they mowed the lawn and worked around the house. But this Saturday, the Smiths were away all day at a wedding, and little Ellen was a terror.

Julie tried playing dolls with her. She tried watching *Sesame Street* on TV with her. Julie even tried taking Ellen outside to play in her sandbox. But nothing was working, and it was only the middle of the morning. Julie brought Ellen to the kitchen and saw several chocolate candy bars on the counter. *That's it,* thought Julie, as she unwrapped the candy bar.

"How about a candy bar?" Julie asked, hoping to get Ellen to stop crying.

Ellen took the candy bar and smiled at Julie. Just as soon as Ellen finished it, she said, "More please, more."

Julie didn't wait. She just unwrapped the candy bars as fast as Ellen wanted them. Not too long afterward, Ellen started scratching a red rash which began spreading all over her body.

Julie knew she had to call Ellen's parents at the reception. But part of her didn't want to. She knew she had not been prudent to let

Ellen eat all those candy bars. It just wasn't wise. If she had practiced temperance and allowed Ellen to have only one candy bar, maybe she would not have gotten the rash.

Now Julie really had to find the fortitude to do what she knew she should. She gathered her inner strength, dialed the reception hall, and waited for Mrs. Smith.

"Mrs. Smith," Julie said when she came to the phone. "I let Ellen eat the candy bars on the counter. She is scratching and has a red rash all over."

There, Julie thought, *it would be perfect justice if they never hire me again.*

"Thank you for calling me, Julie. You should not have let Ellen have all those candy bars but calling me here was very responsible. I'll be right home," Mrs. Smith said.

Why?

1. What virtues did Julie need to overcome her mistake?

   _____

   _____

2. What happens in our lives when we do not practice prudence, justice, fortitude, or temperance?

   _____

   _____

3. Write some examples of how we can grow stronger in prudence, justice, fortitude and temperance.

   _____

   _____

How?

Draw lines to match the virtue on the left with its definition on the right.

Prudence   Inner Strength
Justice   Moderation
Fortitude   Wisdom
Temperance   Fairness

When?

THE TEN COMMANDMENTS

When the Israelites came to the desert of Sinai, they saw a mountain covered with clouds, and from its top, a trumpet sounded loudly. Moses told the people to wait while he went up the mountain, and there the Lord told him how He expected His people to act. They were to tell the truth. They were to love God and honor their parents. They were to say God's name respectfully. They were not to steal or to hurt others. These were God's Ten Commandments.

Moses spent forty days on Mount Sinai, listening to the words of God. The people of Israel thought Moses would never come down, and they began to lose faith in God. They began to worship idols of gold; they feasted and danced to their new manmade god. When Moses returned, he was so angry with the people, he threw down the stone tablets which God had written the Ten Commandments on, and broke them.

Moses returned to Mount Sinai to talk with God and ask His forgiveness for the sins of the people. God restored to the people of Israel the Ten Commandments:

1. I Am the Lord your God. You shall not have other gods before me.
2. You shall not worship any graven image.
3. You shall not take the name of the Lord your God in vain.

4. Remember to keep holy the Sabbath day.
5. Honor your father and your mother.
6. You shall not kill.
7. You shall not commit adultery.
8. You shall not steal.
9. You shall not bear false witness against your neighbor.
10. You shall not covet anything that is your neighbor's.

(Exodus 20:1-17)

Who?

Prudence, justice, fortitude and temperance are the four cardinal virtues. Everyone needs to practice these virtues, as we try to follow God, our Heavenly Father. God created us to be with Him for all eternity. The way this world can have peace and the way we can have peace in our homes and with everyone around us is to live lovingly by the commandments God gave us.

Virtues are the tools we use to follow God's commandments. We practice prudence when we use our consciences. When we are prudent in how we dress, we are practicing wisdom. Prudence tells us when to be careful, so we don't hurt ourselves or our souls. Justice in this world and in heaven is fairness for all. Justice stands for what is right and honorable. If we want God to be just with us, we need to be just with God.

How can we live God's commandments as best we can? We will need to practice fortitude, which means using our inner strength and courage. We need a strong will to do what is right when temptations come. The virtue of temperance also helps us not to go out of control, not to eat too much or give in to selfishness.

Saint Pope John Paul II told the youth at Boston Common on October 1, 1979, "To each one of you I say therefore: 'Heed the call of Christ when you hear Him say to you: "Follow me! Walk in my path! Stand by my side! Remain in my love!' The reason for my mission, for my journey, through the United States is to tell you, to tell everyone – young and old alike – to say to everyone in the name of Christ: 'Come and follow me!'"

We can follow Jesus by practicing prudence, fortitude, temperance and justice.

Where?

All other virtues are built upon the foundation of the cardinal virtues. The more we practice them, the stronger they are in us. The cardinal virtues help us to value what we have, to cheerfully control our whims, and to think about our reasons for spending money. They also help us not to be attached to pleasure, to identify the desires that should be controlled, and to have high ideals that give deep satisfaction rather than superficial pleasures.

Alternate Activities

1. Divide the class into four groups. Give each group one of the cardinal virtues. Role play the best way to practice that virtue.
2. Make a collage from newspaper and/or magazine headlines, half of it showing poor examples of the cardinal virtues and the other half showing good examples of these virtues.
3. Discuss what makes it difficult to practice the cardinal virtues at school, at home, and with friends. What are some of the helps that support living these virtues?
4. Discuss what television shows demonstrate poor examples of prudence, temperance, fortitude, or justice. What television shows set good examples of these virtues?
5. Discuss modern songs with good moral messages that stand up for the cardinal virtues. What songs tear down the virtues of prudence, temperance, fortitude and justice?
6. Play charades with four students trying to act out the four different cardinal virtues.

III. Fruits of the Holy Spirit

A. Charity
B. Joy
C. Peace
D. Patience
E. Kindness
F. Goodness
G. Endurance
H. Mildness
I. Faith
J. Modesty
K. Restraint
L. Chastity

I never realized before how all these virtues and gifts from God help us live each day so much better. When we practice the virtues, God gives us gifts known as the twelve fruits of the Holy Spirit. The Holy Spirit freely showers these gifts on us. They are the results of our good choices. These fruits are like signposts on our path to God. Having and using these fruits lets us know we are on the right path.

Fact number one is: When any one of these fruits is missing, we know one of the virtues is missing: faith, hope, love, prudence, justice, fortitude or temperance. This means to get back the missing fruit (e.g. joy, peace, faith), we must begin again practicing all of the virtues.

Fact number two is: Happiness can only be found by practicing the virtues and the twelve fruits of the Holy Spirit. I discovered some people who only have half of the truth are mistaken when they think they can have happiness without including God in their lives or in their decisions. Only loving God and living the way He shows us can make us truly happy.

Dictionary

Charity: Love, good will, heartfelt caring

Endurance: Long-standing, faithful to the end

Modesty: Freedom and privacy from the gaze of others in dress, thought, sight, hearing and actions

Restraint: Self-control, practicing modesty and chastity

Chastity: Living purity in body, mind and soul

My Notes

_____

_____

_____

_____

_____

What?

A FUN FAMILY

The Hennings family had only moved into town about one month earlier, and already their home was a favorite spot for neighboring teenagers. No one could put their finger on why they liked to go there so much, they just did. They didn't have a lot of fancy things. People simply liked being around them and liked how they felt after visiting the Hennings. Their family wasn't so different, they just had a lot of joy. And for having six kids, ages five to seventeen, they sure had a lot of peace and love in the house.

Mrs. Hennings was fun to talk to and had an interesting way of looking at things, like homework, for example. With a twinkle in her eye she could patiently explain math, as though it were no problem. Once when I had worn out Mom and Dad's brain on a math teaser problem, Mrs. Hennings, with her kind spirit, spent hours with me until I got it right. She didn't have to help me. She had enough kids of her own. But she stuck to it, with that endurance of hers, and helped me anyway.

The whole family shared that mildness. We noticed that they attended the same Mass we did on Saturday evenings. Mom pointed out to me after one of the Masses, when the three older Hennings teenagers were going out for the evening, how they were dressed modestly. *Modesty means a lot to Mom*, I thought. Then I thought, *It really means a lot to me, too. What I wear does say a lot about myself. Modesty is my right to privacy.* I found myself thinking about chastity, keeping myself pure in body and soul. Those Hennings teenagers always practiced self-control when others were around. It was fun to go to their parties at their home and not have to worry about what room you walked into or what you might find there. I found myself glad and proud to be their friend.

Why?

1. What is it like to have a good friend or know a good family who brings out the best in you?

   _____

   _____

2. What are some of the fruits of the Holy Spirit that the Hennings family had?

   _____

   _____

3. What made it so comfortable at the Hennings home when they had parties?

_____

_____

How?

The twelve fruits of the Holy Spirit are gifts from God. The Holy Spirit is the third person of the Trinity, which includes God the Father, Jesus God's Son, and the Holy Spirit, the active Love between the Father and the Son.

Draw twelve large fruits (e.g. on a tree, in a garden, or in a basket). Then write the name of one of the gifts in each fruit. They are: charity, joy, peace, patience, kindness, goodness, endurance, mildness, faith, modesty, restraint and chastity.

When?

A PURE AND HOLY CHILD

Joachim and Anne were the grandparents of Jesus, but they were very old before God sent them our Blessed Mother as a child. Joachim and Anne were rich and faithful Jews. Each year at the Temple, before Mary was born to them, Joachim made a double offering to make up for his sins. One day when Joachim made his offering, the Jewish elders told him, "It is not right for you to offer first gifts, for you have begotten no offspring in Israel."

Joachim was very sad and went to the desert to fast and pray. Anne also prayed in her home. There was no greater misfortune for a Jewish person than to be childless. Anne promised God, if He would send her a child, she would bring it up in the faith. She also promised God the child would serve Him all the days of its life. God heard the prayers of Joachim and Anne and sent them a baby girl, Mary.

In gratitude to God for the blessing of a daughter, Joachim and Anne brought Mary to the Temple when she was around three years old. At the Temple she was accepted into the special group of virgins, consecrated to God, and received spiritual lessons.

The desires of the world, vanity, immodest dress, and sin never touched her pure soul. She was preserved virginal, body and soul, so that she would be the loving, pure, first "tabernacle: of Jesus, God-made man on earth.

Mary treasured her purity and her virginity. Even when God sent Jesus to her, and she was married to Joseph, Mary was filled with all the fruits of the Holy Spirit.

Who?

When we were baptized, our souls were washed clean from Original Sin. Our souls were pure, and God gave us the gifts of faith, hope and love. As we grow, we practice the virtues of prudence, fortitude, temperance and justice. We strengthen our union with Jesus each time we receive Him in the Sacraments of Reconciliation and Holy Communion. God loves us so much that when we follow Him and obey His Ten Commandments out of love for Him, He floods us with His gifts of the Holy Spirit.

The twelve gifts of the Holy Spirit help us to be happy and healthy in body and soul while we are on earth. God gave each one of us all these gifts. It is His intent that we use them.

The gifts of charity, joy, peace, patience, kindness and goodness are easier to understand than the others, because we might be more familiar with them. As with all the gifts, the more we share them to others, the more they are multiplied back to us. We are truly loving when we are caring more about the other person than ourselves. There is a wonderful feeling we get inside us when we practice mildness. It is especially nice when others are also good and mild toward us. These fruits help us not to go out of control when we don't get what we want, when and how we want it. Endurance means patiently waiting, like the friend that will always be there. We practice patient endurance and use our faith in God when we have courage to learn what God expects of us in our behavior. It takes courage by using faith and endurance to stand by God's Word, day after day and year after year. God always rewards us for being faithful to Him, with many more treasures than the world gives.

The last three fruits of the Holy Spirit, modesty, restraint (self-control), and chastity (purity in body and soul), are gifts God gives us, which He does not want us to abuse. Imagine if we gave our friend a gift, and he or she stepped all over it. That would be an abuse of the gift. Instead, we want to treasure God's gifts because they are special helps for us.

Modesty gives us the privacy to keep things to ourselves that ought to be kept to ourselves. We can be modest in the way we dress, in our language, in what we choose to watch at the movies or on TV, or in the music we listen to. Modesty protects us from the gaze of others, gives us respect for our bodies and the bodies of others, and keeps us pure, like Mary and Jesus.

The gift of restraint helps us practice self-control with modesty and gives us strength not to go places or do things with others that we know are sinful and against God.

Chastity is the gift that calls us to live with purity, truth and sincerity, whether we are single children, teenagers or married adults.

Where?

The twelve gifts of the Holy Spirit are positive helps for us, which we can be proud to have and practice. We will sometimes hear the world tell us not to have these wonderful gifts of faith, or modesty, or chastity. But we know the Holy Spirit, who is full of love, gives the very best to us. These fruits get stronger when we practice them.

Alternate Activities

1. Hold a prayer service, using scriptures involving the fruits of the Holy Spirit.
2. Have each student write four sentences on only one of the twelve fruits of the Holy Spirit. Share the writings.
3. Think of twelve different occupations in which the worker would need at least one of the twelve fruits. Use all the fruits.
4. Have students each write a short story using all twelve fruits. Stories must not slander anyone and must have integrity.
5. Divide the class in half. Have a debate on why the twelve fruits of the Holy Spirit are necessary in life.
6. Create a poster using symbols for each of the fruits.

IV. Seven Capital Sins

A. Pride
B. Covetousness
C. Lust
D. Anger
E. Gluttony
F. Envy
G. Sloth

The puzzle about morality is beginning to come together for me. Morality is when we use the virtues and character God gave us to make good choices for our thoughts and actions. God created each one of us and everything in the world for His glory. He also created the order of nature, the sun, the moon, and the stars, to give us days and nights and the seasons.

When God created people for His world, He created us to live in a certain order, too. Since the first sin of Adam and Eve, all people have a fallen nature. As hard as we try, we can't live without making mistakes. If we freely choose a thought or an action that we know is against the love of God, then this mistake is a sin. This is because we know it would hurt God, but we do it anyway. Jesus always forgives us of any sin in the Sacrament of Reconciliation, to make things right with God, our loving Father.

Fact number one is: A half-truth about sin says there is no such thing as sin, that you have to do what is right for you, and not think about what God wants, even if it bothers your conscience.

Fact number two is: Another half-truth is that we do not need the Sacrament of Reconciliation anymore.

Dictionary

Pride: (the sin) Arrogance, conceit, superiority complex

Covetousness: Overly desiring something belonging to another

20

Lust: An intense craving or desire, especially sexual

Anger: Violent and strong displeasure, wrath

Gluttony: To eat excessively

Envy: Resentment and jealousy over possessions or achievements

Sloth: Laziness, sluggishness, not exerting energy

My Notes

_____

_____

_____

_____

_____

What?

NOT SO POPULAR

The students in Mrs. Taylor's class all got along fairly well, except for Ruffy. No one liked him. Maybe it was the way he always strutted into the room, so proud and arrogant. Or maybe it was because as soon as someone showed up with something new, he had to go out and get something like it, only better. He wanted everything people had, and if he couldn't get it or one better, it just drove him crazy.

He even wanted things he shouldn't have wanted. He had a passion for not just getting things, but people – girls. Ruffy tried to fit in with the boys by bragging about how many girlfriends he had and what he did on his dates. The girls who had strong characters wouldn't go out with him at all, even though he was on the football team.

"Hey Jen," Ruffy said as he cozied up to her desk. "Want to go to the movies with me tonight?"

"I've already made other plans. Sorry," Jen answered. Why did he have to ask her in front of her friends? The truth was, football team or not, Jen knew how Ruffy treated girls. She had respect for herself, even if Ruffy did not.

"You did the right thing," Dotty whispered to Jen. "I wish I had told him no when he asked me out last week. He said we could watch TV at his house, but when we got there, his parents were working. It's no wonder he's a quarterback on the football team. You should see how he pigs out. And what a pig! He had his clothes and books all strewn all over their living room. When I realized what was going on, I just left as fast as I could. What a temper! When I said I had to leave, he took a fit right there in the front yard. You definitely did the right thing."

Why?

1. There are seven sins that Ruffy committed. Can you name them?

   _____

   _____

2. Did Ruffy's way of life really make him popular? Why?

   _____

   _____

3. Can Ruffy change his ways or is he stuck with his bad habits? How?

   _____

   _____

How?

Write down the best way to say "NO" when you want to have something, or do something, but you know you shouldn't. How do you turn down desserts, candy, invitations and material things when you know you should?

_____

_____

When?

DAVID AND BATHSHEBA

God loved the Israelite people very much, even though they would sometimes sin and turn away from Him. God allowed them to go through difficult times so that His people would realize their mistake and turn back to Him. Still God loved them and would always take them back. He even promised His people that, from the line of King David, He would send a Savior.

One evening David, King of Israel, was strolling on the palace roof. He noticed a very beautiful woman bathing in the garden next to the palace wall. Her name was Bathsheba.

Since King David was walking on the palace roof, he could not easily see over the wall that divided their properties. King David knew that Bathsheba was married, but he watched her anyway. King David was infatuated with her and asked his messengers to bring her to him.

God sent the prophet Nathan to King David, Nathan said to David, "The God of Israel says this, 'I anointed you King over Israel and I delivered you from the hands of Saul who wanted to kill you.' Why have you shown contempt for God, doing what displeases Him?"

King David answered Nathan, "I have sinned against God. I am sorry for offending God."

Nathan said to him, "God forgives you your sin." (2 Samuel 11:1-3, 12:7, 12:13)

Who?

In Rome, on December 20, 1978, Saint Pope John Paul II told young people that sin is a transgression (to go beyond the limits) of God's commandment. He said:

"We know that by sin, the Lord is offended, friendship with Him is broken, His grace is lost, and one strays from the right path, heading for ruin. God, by means of His commandments, teaches us in practice how we must behave in order to live in a dignified, human, and serene way. With the commandments, God instills in us respect for or parents and superiors, respect for all life, respect for the body and love, respect for what belongs to others, and respect for truth. Sin is to ignore, trample upon, and transgress these wise and useful rules, which the Lord gave us; that is why it is disorder and ruin!"

Sometimes sin looks attractive to us, because we want to have something or to do something we should not have or do. When we are honest with ourselves and choose sin, we realize it is a lack of respect for ourselves, others, and especially God, who loves us so very much. Sin separates us so much from God that if we are in serious sin, we cannot go to heaven with this sin on our souls. Because God loves us, even when we are sinning, He sent us Jesus, who became one of us and died on the cross to wipe sin away. All we have to do is make peace with God in the Sacrament of Reconciliation.

But the easiest way of dealing with sin is to learn to say "NO" in the first place. Each time we say "NO" to that dessert or candy bar we want or that piece of clothing we really don't need, we get stronger in mastering our desires. Imagine if we constantly ate chocolate cream pies morning, noon and night, simply because we felt we wanted to. By learning to say "NO" to little things along the way, when the time comes, we will know how to say "NO" to important things later on.

Where?

God gave us the theological virtue of hope. There is always hope. When we sin, we can always turn back to the loving arms of God, our Father. Sin is a deliberate turning away from God. Any time we break one of the Ten Commandments, we sin. God has also written His law in our hearts. Our consciences will tell us when we are not walking with God the way we should. God is always calling us closer to Him. At times we will have to choose God's way over the world's way. If we practice the theological virtues and the cardinal virtues, we can overcome the seven capital sins.

Alternate Activities

1. Put the capital sins on trial. Set up a court room. Choose someone to be "God" as the judge. Choose the jury and attorneys for and against the capital sins. Are they guilty of breaking the Ten Commandments? Which ones?
2. Hold a prayer service with candles, scripture readings, prayers of petition, and thanksgiving for God's unconditional love. This could even be done, with permission, in the church.
3. What do TV, radio and movies have to say about the seven capital sins?
4. Discuss why the seven capital sins do not make people "really" happy.
5. Discuss how the seven capital sins can be disguised as good things.
6. Debate the reality of sin in the world. Is sin real? What affects of sin can be seen in the world, in governments, in advertising, and in our neighborhoods? What is the remedy for sin?

V. The Opposite Virtues

A. **Humility**
B. **Generosity**
C. **Chastity**
D. **Meekness**
E. **Temperance**
F. **Brotherly Love**
G. **Diligence**

I've just discovered the seven opposite virtues are the remedy to the seven capital sins. We will not fall into sin when we are tempted if we practice these virtues. It's like uncovering the biggest secret yet! I feel much better about things when I know I've got the answers. Then I know I'm in control and tempting situations are not controlling me. I feel much better after the temptation situation is over, when I practice these opposite virtues, because then I have no regrets. Practicing the opposite virtues is an added bonus, because we again are showered with the twelve fruits of the Holy Spirit.

Fact number one is: It is a half-truth to say only cowards use virtues. Some people say it is better to show anger rather than meekness or materialism rather than generosity. The truth is, cowards choose to sin rather than use virtues because they are afraid to say "NO" to sin.

Fact number two is: It is a half-truth to say it is more popular to sin than to use virtues. Friends want true friends who stick up for honesty, integrity and virtues. When we commit sins, we take unfair advantage of others by selfishness and greed. This does not make us popular.

Dictionary

Humility: Truth and knowledge of who we are, unpretending

Generosity: A giving spirit, helping with time and materials

Chastity: Purity in body and soul, modesty in dress and conduct

Meekness: Gentleness, kindness in spirit

Temperance: Self-control, moderation in food or passions, orderliness

Brotherly Love: Affectionate caring, heartwarming concern

Diligence: Hard work, industriousness, constant effort

What?

MOTHER TERESA

When Agnes Gouxha Bojaxhlu was twelve years old, she already knew she wanted to spend her life serving God. Although Agnes' family was very poor, their family life centered on God. The whole family attended Mass every morning at the Church of the Sacred Heart.

On September 25, 1928, Agnes was 18 years old and said a tearful goodbye to her family. She never saw her family again. She studied English and went to India, staying with the Loreto Sister's Convent. There Agnes took her first vows of poverty, chastity and obedience, and chose the name Sister Teresa in honor of Saint Theresa, the patron saint of missionaries.

Starvation and misery were everywhere she looked. Hundreds of bodies were in the streets, and she wanted to help them. Sister Teresa received medical training and learned how to give shots, set broken bones and care for diseases. Every day she worked with the sick and dying until late into the evening. Soon many young women, some from very wealthy families gave up everything that had to help India's poorest people.

In 1950 Sister Teresa became Mother Superior of a new order called the Missionaries of Charity. She also started a children's home for sick and abandoned children.

In December 1979, Mother Teresa traveled to Oslo, Norway to receive the Nobel Peace Prize for her work with the poor. When she arrived, the weather was freezing, but she wore all she had, a simple sari, sandals and a sweater. That night, the Norwegian Nobel

Committee presented Mother Teresa with a check worth $190,000, which she said she would use for homes, "because I believe that love begins at home; and if we can create a home for the poor, I think that more and more love will spread," Mother Teresa said.

On September 2, 2016, Pope Francis declared Blessed Teresa – Mother Teresa – a saint at a canonization service held in front of St Peter's Basilica in Vatican City, Rome.

Why?

1. Explain specific instances when Mother Teresa practiced humility, generosity, chastity, meekness, temperance, brotherly love and diligence.
2. What was so important about Mother Teresa's work that the world recognized her by giving her the Nobel Peace Prize?
3. What helped Mother Teresa live such a virtuous life?

How?

Draw a line from the virtue that is the remedy for each of the seven capital sins.

Temperance	Pride
Diligence	Covet
Brotherly Love	Lust
Humility	Anger
Chastity	Gluttony
Meekness	Envy
Generosity	Sloth

When?

KING SOLOMON

King David had a son named Solomon. As he grew, he pleased God greatly when he prayed for wisdom rather than riches or a long life. Solomon became known as one of the wisest men in all of Israel and became king after his father died. He wrote many proverbs, known as true sayings, about seven hundred years before Jesus was born. King Solomon used the wisdom God gave him and loved to write about practicing virtues. The words God gave King Solomon to tell the people almost three thousand years ago are just as true today. Here are some things he wrote about the seven capital sins and the opposite virtues:

Pride: "Pride comes first, disgrace comes after, with the humble is wisdom found. The arrogant heart is disgusting to God, be sure it will not go unpunished."

Covetousness: "The godless are forever coveting; the virtuous man gives without ever refusing. The generous man has many to court his favor; to one who gives, everyone is friend."

Lust: "Their virtuous conduct sets honest men free; treacherous men are imprisoned by their own desires. He who seduces honest men to evil ways will fall into his own pit."

Anger: "A bad-tempered man starts fights, a man who gets angry easily is a great cause of sin. A mild answer turns away anger; sharp words stir up anger."

Gluttony: "Do not be one of those forever drinking wine nor one of those who gorge themselves with meat; for the drunkard and glutton rob themselves of strength of character."

Envy: "The life of the body is a peaceful heart, but envy is a cancer to the bones. Do not let your heart be envious of sinners but be steady every day in the fear of the Lord."

Sloth: "The idle man has no game to roast; diligence (hard work) is a man's most precious possession. The slack hand brings poverty, but the diligent hand brings wealth."

Who?

Ever since the fall of Adam and Eve, there has been sin in the world. But we are never forced to sin. God gives us the wisdom, like Solomon's, to practice virtues.

Humility helps us know ourselves. Saint Theresa of Avila said, "Humility means walking in the truth; pride means walking in falsehood."

Generosity with our heart helps us act unselfishly and not want, or covet, what everyone else has. Today covetousness is also called materialism.

Chastity helps us keep our bodies and souls pure for God and save sex for the Sacrament of Marriage. God calls some men and women to give a complete gift of themselves to Christ in the priesthood and religious life.

Meekness is gentleness and kindness of spirit and gives us an alternative to anger.

Temperance is when we are in control of pleasurable things, so situations or our feelings are not in control of us.

Brotherly Love is true love for everyone and has no room for envy.

Diligence keeps us on our toes, makes us appreciate a job well done, and shuts the door on laziness.

Where?

Jesus and our Blessed Mother Mary are perfect examples of people who are successful in practicing all of the virtues. We need to be humble even when great things are asked of us. Generosity helps us not place too much importance on things, which others, or the store has, and to use things wisely. Chastity is our privacy and freedom to keep ourselves pure, not to become slaves to sin, and saves us from becoming objects to be used by other people. Meekness allows us the gentle spirit to deal with others and gives us a choice in our attitude. Temperance helps us put on the brakes when we want too much of a good thing. Brotherly love is the caring and concern we show for all of God's people, out of respect for them. Diligence keeps the electricity flowing in our will power and determination when we are tempted to laziness.

Alternate Activities

1. Divide the class into two groups. Give one group the first three opposite virtues, and the second group the last four opposite virtues. Discuss when they saw these virtues used (e.g., friends, TV, movies)
2. In addition to Saint Teresa, discuss modern day "opposite" virtuous heroes.
3. Discuss what it means to be a modern-day saint. Find scriptures in the New Testament that call us all to be saints. Discuss the royal priesthood.
4. Divide the class into two groups. Brainstorm which theological or cardinal virtue is the root of each of each of the opposite virtues.
5. Brainstorm on the blackboard three positive results of each of the opposite virtues.
6. Hold a scripture service by reading passages that demonstrate each of the opposite virtues.

VI. Friendship

A. **Mutual Respect**
B. **Sincerity**
C. **Loyalty**
D. **Faithfulness**
E. **Honesty**
F. **Purity**
G. **Self-Esteem**

Do you have any clue about what I have just dug up? Friendship means different things to different people. Some people have certain expectations of what friendship is and isn't. I had no idea friendship could be so confusing. Let's check the facts.

It's a fact that friends are sincere, loyal and honest with each other. These are the characteristics of true friends. This is why friends do not use one another, encourage one another to get into trouble, or hurt one another. The mutual respect they have for each other won't allow this. Friends are for their own self-esteem and try to build up the self-esteem of their friends, too.

Another fact is that our friends need our faithfulness to them and to God. When our friendship with God is strong, and we share that with our friends, then we have the strongest kind of friendships. God is truth and love, two of the strongest qualities in friendship.

Fact number one is: True friends care just as much about the other person as they do about themselves.

Fact number two is: True friends never manipulate one another.

Dictionary

Purity: Clean, chaste, innocent, blameless, free from anything that weakens or pollutes

Sincerity: Honest, genuine, free from deceit

Loyalty: Allegiance, fidelity, truth

Respect: Reverence, consideration, appreciation

Faithfulness: Trustworthiness, truth, loyalty

My Notes

_____

_____

_____

_____

_____

What?

TRUE FRIENDSHIP

People said it was rare. Some said it was special. But all Carrie and Robbie knew was that, even though they were thirteen-year-old twins, they were the best of friends. They enjoyed being together and laughed at the same things; and when they messed up doing their chores at home, they even got in trouble together.

Sometimes they got on each other's nerves, as only a brother and sister can do. Yet, despite everything, when they patched things up, they had great mutual respect for each other. Sure they had other friends, like Ellie and Dan, but they were loyal to each other, no matter what.

"Do you know what I heard about Carrie?" Ellie said to Robbie. "She couldn't sink a hoop at last night's basketball game to save her life. The kids were saying you probably dipped her hands in glue before the game!"

Kidding or not, no one talked about his sister like that, not to his face anyway.

"Look, Ellie, basketball is about teamwork. Last week Carrie sank every hoop she shot. She was just giving other teammates a chance to score, that's all," Robbie answered quickly.

"But we were all expecting her to bring us to the championship, and she let us down," Dan added.

"Let *you* down?" Robbie demanded hotly. "Both of you are supposed to be our friends. You are letting *Carrie* down. Your expectations about her are out of line. If you would honestly examine your own motives, you will find they are not too pure. You are more interested in your own selves than Carrie."

With that Robbie headed for home with his head held high. He believed in his sister and himself enough to stand up for her when the going got tough.

Why?

1. What are some of the characteristics of friendship?

   _____

   _____

2. Do true friends place unrealistic expectations on each other or pressure each other?

   _____

   _____

3. What are the best ways to enjoy a pure, sincere and loyal friendship?

   _____

   _____

How?

Write three characteristics you like most about your friends (e.g., mutual respect, sincerity, loyalty, faithfulness, purity, modesty, generosity, optimism, fortitude, orderly, flexibility, patience, understanding, trustworthy) **and three characteristics you like least** (e.g., rudeness, insincerity, being demanding, selfishness). **Do Not mention names.**

Characteristics I like most:

1. _____
2. _____
3. _____

Characteristics I like least:

1. _____
2. _____
3. _____

When?

DAVID AND JONATHAN

As a young man, before David was king, he used his talent to play the harp for King Saul. The music would soothe King Saul when he was depressed. King Saul's son Jonathan and David became best friends. Jonathan gave David his fancy robe and tunic and, also, his bow, belt and sword.

God blessed David. But King Saul became jealous and angry when David won in battle because the people began to like David better than the king. In an attempt to try to kill David, King Saul threw his spear at him, but he missed.

As much as it hurt Jonathan's heart to send David away, Jonathan cared more for his good friend.

"You must leave this city, David. Get away from the king," Jonathan pleaded.

"No matter where we are, we will always be best friends forever," David answered. (1 Samuel 18-20)

Who?

Friendship arises out of virtue, and it grows as virtue grows. There is no friendship where there is no virtue. In friendship we care more about the other person, about sharing, than ourselves or selfishness. Friendship is more than being sociable, more than loving our neighbor. It's a deeper, closer, special relationship. Friends share common interests, experiences, feelings, thoughts, and plans.

Another sign of friendship is that friends try to improve one another, looking out for their best interest, and care for each other's physical, emotional and spiritual wellbeing. True friends are honest with each other, sincere, loyal, faithful and pure. The reason friendship fosters purity in heart, mind and soul is that a true friend would never place the other in a compromising position. That means as friends, we would never ask anything of our friends that would rob their self-esteem or place expectations on them beyond that which God wants. A true friend would never lead the other to sin and wants his or her friend to reach heaven as much as he or she wants to.

All of the theological virtues of faith, hope and love; all of the cardinal virtues of prudence, justice, fortitude and temperance; all of the twelve fruits of the Holy Spirit, including modesty and chastity; and all of the opposite virtues grow stronger as our friendships grow. The world is waiting for strong friendships. The world is waiting for true love.

Saint Pope John Paul II said, "For youth is the time for new contacts, new companionships, and friendships, in a circle wider than the family alone ... In this way we learn to know other human beings. In order to become more fully human through our capacity for self-giving, for becoming men and women for others. Our cities need souls if they are to become a true home for human beings. You, the young people, must give it this soul. And how do you do this? By loving each other."

Where?

God strengthens our friendships when we practice the virtues. True friends share mutual respect and genuine caring. Friendship values the life and wellbeing of the other before his or her own desires. True friendship is motivated by generosity, giving, and would not steal the reputation or self-esteem of the other at any cost.

Alternate Activities

1. Divide the class into two panels. One discusses the characteristics of acquaintances. The other discusses the characteristics of friendships.
2. Brainstorm the best part of friendships and what makes friendships difficult.
3. Role play what friends can do to make their friendships deeper and what can harm friendships.
4. Discuss ways to avoid or get out of situations when someone pretends to be a friend and the other person becomes uncomfortable because his/her chastity is challenged.
5. Discuss the differences between what makes a person popular and what makes a person a friend. Discuss negative peer pressure and its affects.
6. Have a book review from their reading that dealt with friendships. Why did they like or dislike the books.

VII. Decision Making

A. **Free Will**
B. **Coercion**
C. **Responsibility**
D. **Exploitation**
E. **Peer Pressure**
F. **Character**

Knowing the whole truth makes decision making that much easier. My friends have been telling me that the hardest kinds of decisions to make are when people around me, or on TV, or in other programs tell me something is okay when I know it's really *not* okay.

One thing to remember is that we also use free will in all our decisions. No one can force us to do what we know we shouldn't. If someone tries to force you to do something you do not want to, **tell someone you trust**. Someone trying to force you to so something wrong or immoral is pressuring you by coercion. This is also called negative peer pressure, and manipulation. We can show responsibility for ourselves and others when we show strength of character and live the virtues.

Fact number one is: True friends will never pressure you to smoke, take drugs, or do anything that will not keep your bodies pure before the Sacrament of Marriage, or hurt you in any way.

Fact number two is: You can also say "NO" to any situation you need to. Some people are afraid to say "NO" to bad situations, but saying "NO" to temptations makes your character stronger; and you'll feel better.

Dictionary

Free Will: Choices we make on our own

Coercion: Forcing someone to do something against his or her free will

Human Respect: Caring about what other people think

Exploitation: Using people without their free will for the benefit of others

Good Character: Moral excellence, a good reputation

My Notes

_____

_____

_____

_____

_____

What?

MATT'S DECISION

When Fingers, the name Frank was known by in New York City, moved to Sturbridge, he was accustomed to being the leader of a gang. He didn't have any friends in New York City; and he didn't have any in Sturbridge either. His first day at junior high school, he wasted no time in trying to set up his "business" as usual.

Fingers tried to make use of his time in the hall to back kids up against the lockers, threaten to meet them at a particular store after school, and start up his business of having kids steal for him. Fingers would never steal himself. He would just turn around and sell the things, at least that's what happened back where he came from. Then he would buy beer. He thought drinking and parties made kids popular.

But his first day at his new school went very differently. As he tried to back Matt up to the locker, Matt stepped toward Frank. Matt never backed up on the basketball court or in the weight room at the gym, and he was not going to back up now.

"Look," Matt said stepping up to Frank's face. "I challenge you to a little one-on-one at the hoop after school. Let's see if those muscles are as good as they look."

Matt didn't know what this new guy was capable of, but no one was going to coerce or force him to do something, especially something that could get him bounced off the team. He did not care one bit about human respect, that is, the opinions others had and peer pressure. Matt was not accustomed to being exploited, that is, being used for someone else's benefit. No one "used" him – no one.

"Are you serious?" Frank asked. No one had ever taken the time to invite him to anything before. "Ya. I'll be there," he said.

Why?

1. How did Frank and Matt each use their free will?

_____

_____

2. How would others have been hurt by Frank's coercion and exploitation, stealing for his benefit?

_____

_____

3. What is strength of character, and how can we strengthen it? How is human respect harmful when it comes to peer pressure? Do people think more of us if we do illegal or immoral things?

_____

_____

How?

Write down brand names of items or companies who treat people as "things" in the media (e.g., soft drinks, clothing, products). What other message are the advertisers sending?

Brand Name:	What's the message:
1. _____	1. _____
2. _____	2. _____
3. _____	3. _____

When?

SUSANNA'S INNOCENCE

In the days of the young prophet Daniel, there lived a beautiful, married woman named Susanna. She loved God and her Jewish faith very much. Her husband Joakim was rich, had a large garden attached to his house, and would often be visited by Jewish leaders, since he was held in greater respect than any other man. Two wicked elders and judges for the Jewish people visited often because they lusted for Susanna and tried to coerce her to let them have their way with her. They even told Susanna if she didn't give in to them, they would accuse her in public of being with a younger man, which meant she would be put to death.

"I am trapped," Susanna said when they cornered her along in the garden. "If I agree, that means my death if I resist, I cannot get away from you. But I will sin in the eyes of the Lord."

The next day a meeting was held at the house of Joakim. The two evil judges arrived, lied to everyone about her being with a younger man, and determined to have Susanna put to death.

"Eternal God, you know all secrets and everything before it happens. You know they have given false evidence against me," Susanna prayed.

The Lord heard her prayer and stirred Daniel's heart to come forth. Daniel called everyone together and asked that the two judges be kept apart. To the first judge Daniel asked, "Since you saw them so clearly, under which tree did you see them?"

He replied, "Under the Mastic Tree."

The second judge was brought out and answered, "Under an oak tree."

Susanna's life was saved. As for the judges, they received the same penalty intended for Susanna. (Daniel 13:1-64)

Who?

God made all Creation, including us, for His honor and glory. He made us with our human bodies, but He also made us with spiritual and immortal souls, which will live on forever. All decisions we make will affect our relationship with God each day. We need to take responsibility and use our free will in a way that builds up the virtues, our families, and our world n the way God asks us.

It takes a strong, courageous person to stand up for what is right. We need to use the common sense God gives us to make decisions. Living as a Christian young person means walking in the way God asks us to, because we love God and know that He loves us more than we can ever imagine. This means sometimes saying "NO" to ourselves to things that at first seem popular, or self-indulgent, when we know these things will hurt us physically, emotionally or spiritually.

Following God's commandments gives us true freedom. Following false ideals makes us slaves to selfishness, greed, and everything against God. We need to use our free will to make our decisions, never being coerced or forced, to do the things we know are wrong. We need to learn not to be exploited, meaning to be taken advantage of, by advertisements, songs, or sometimes even friends. It is important not to make decisions based on human respect, what other people will think. Our decisions must be based on what God expects of us.

When Saint Pope John Paul II spoke to the French youth on June 1, 1980, he challenged them to "form" their consciences, not to "deform" them. He said, "Moral permissiveness does not make men happy. The consumer society does not make men happy. It has never done so."

Where?

God made the world, the universe, and us. God created us in a world that uses time and order according to His divine plan. God also created us with free will. We are totally free to make moral decisions, to follow God's commandments, and to love God, our Heavenly Father. We are also free to choose actions and thoughts against God. God respects us too much to coerce us, or force us to love Him. God is counting on us, to use the intelligence He gave us, to think and act responsibly, to show others our strength of character, and not to give in to human respect. God's grace will always help us to make good decisions. Heaven is God's reward for us after a life full of good decisions. If and when we make mistakes and sin, God always forgives us in the Sacrament of Reconciliation. This keeps our relationship with God healthy.

Alternative Activities

1. On the blackboard, as a class, write down five sentences friends would never say to one another to coerce or force them to do something.
2. Brainstorm the best ways to make a decision. How do you decide what to do? How do you ask for advice? Who should we ask? How do we know if we should follow their advice? How do you tell if the advice is good?
3. Make a large poster, half with pictures or sayings coercing someone to do or think or wear something, and the other half with pictures or sayings of responsibility.
4. Discuss ways to stand up to peer pressure and the opinions of others.

5. Divide the class in half. Each group tries to come up with the most ways to support friends in good decision making.
6. List ways to remedy poor decisions. What can be done to make up with others? How do we fix sinful behaviors? In what sacrament is Jesus waiting for us? Do we have a new beginning after Jesus forgives us?

Teacher's Objectives

Appendix A

I. THEOLOGICAL VIRTUES

A. Faith
B. Hope
C. Love

Students should be able to:

1. Define the three theological virtues: faith, hope and love.
2. Know that these virtues are "infused," or received, directly from God.
3. Know that God gives these three virtues as gifts and God is their ultimate end.
4. Know that these virtues, as all other virtues, grow in strength the more they are used, and diminish when they are ignored.
5. Understand and give examples of living faith, hope and love in their lives.

Background for the Teacher

FAITH: Peter Kreeft, Boston College theologian and author of *Back to Virtue*, states that the fall of Adam and Eve was a fall of faith. Only because of their lack of faith did they disobey. "Faith or its lack is the root cause of obedience or disobedience, faithfulness or sin. Sin is faithfulness, infidelity ... the object of faith is God, not ideas about God ... Unless you believe, you will not understand ... faith first ... Faith is more active than reason. The word yes is the simplest word there is."

HOPE: Kreeft says that "hope is faith directed to the future. God is the object of hope. God's revelation, in the form of His many promises (over three hundred different promises in scripture) ...express the structure of hope. Hope means that my deepest values, wants, demands, longings, and ideals are not meaningless subjective blips … but are like radar … of objective reality."

LOVE: "Agape … that new, specific, radical kind of love that the world simply had not seen before Christ … look at Christ dying for us on the Cross. That is the best definition of love in the world," Kreeft writes. "God is not asking for a bit of room in our heart, in our soul, or in our mind, for just a share in our life: He wants it all – not just a little love, some part of our life, but all we have got," Francis Fernandez says in his meditation from *In Conversation with God*.

"The three theological virtues are a single plant. Faith is its root. Hope is its stalk, its life thrust. Love is its fruit. The plant is God's own life in us … Life offers us only one failure: to miss this mark, to miss God. Faith, hope and charity ae the hands that receive God," Kreeft explains.

Prayer to Jesus Christ Crucified

My good and dear Jesus, I kneel before you, asking you most earnestly to engrave upon my heart a deep and lively faith, hope and charity, with true repentance to make amends. As I reflect upon your five wounds, and dwell upon them with deep compassion and grief, I recall, good Jesus, the words of the prophet David spoke long ago concerning yourself: they have pierced my hands and my feet, they have counted all my bones!

AMEN

Teacher's Objectives

Appendix B

II. CARDINAL VIRTUES

A. **Prudence**
B. **Justice**

C. **Fortitude**
D. **Temperance**

Students should be able to:

1. Define the four cardinal virtues: prudence, justice, fortitude and temperance.
2. Know that these virtues are "acquired" virtues, that is, we can get stronger in them simply by practicing them.
3. Know that these are natural "moral" virtues.
4. Understand and give examples of practicing prudence, justice, fortitude and temperance.

Background for the Teacher

PRUDENCE: "In his work and dealings with other people, the prudent person gathers information which he assesses in the light of the right standards: he weighs the favorable and unfavorable consequences for himself and others prior to making a decision, and then he acts or refrains from acting, in keeping with the decision he has made," Dr. David Isaacs says, director of the School of Education at the University of Navarre, Spain, and author of *Character Building*. "One of the problems related to this virtue is what we might call "false prudence." Isaacs writes as he quotes Saint Josemaria Escriva de Balaguer y Albas, "Which 'is at the service of selfishness and is expert in using the best means to achieve warped ends.'" Isaacs continues, "Imprudence – which includes precipitance, thoughtlessness, and inconstancy – is very much connected with failure to control one's passions."

JUSTICE: "A just person strives constantly to give others what is their due, so that they can fulfill their duties and exercise their rights as persons (right to life, to cultural and moral goods, to material goods), as parents, as children, as citizens, as regulates our relationship with God and with others ... it calls for simplicity, sincerity and gratitude ... and brings peace," Isaacs says.

Fortitude: "In situations which make it difficult to improve, a courageous person resists harmful influences, withstands difficulties, and strives to act positively to overcome obstacles and undertake great deeds," Isaacs states. He adds, "It is not a matter of performing superhuman actions of discovering unexplored territory, of rescuing fifty children from a fire ... What we can, and must do is to transform the simple things of everyday into a chain of efforts, courageous acts, which may indeed become great and heroic, an expression of love ... It is worth reminding ourselves that children need to be convinced that their lives have a purpose, that however insignificant and useless one's life may seem, each individual las an inalienable mission to glorify God ... Anyone who is selfish and unwilling to improve, who seeks only pleasure, is not motivated to develop the virtue of fortitude, for he is indifferent to good."

TEMPERANCE: Moderation. Self-control. "Now what about greed? Is that virtue? No. Capitalism is wicked because it fosters greed, materialism, consumerism ... But are material things (or our God-given gift of our sexuality) evil in themselves? ... No ... We should desire and get and use just what we naturally and truly need (at the appropriate time), not what the ad men tell us and sell us ... Material things (and our passions) are our servants, not our masters," Kreeft says in *Back to Virtues*.

Prayer: A Spirit to Know You

(St. Benedict of Nursia)

Gracious and holy Father, please give me:

intellect to understand you, reason to discern you,

a spirit to know you, a heart to meditate on you, ears to hear you, eyes to see you, a tongue to proclaim you, a way of life pleasing to you,

patience to wait for you, and perseverance to look for you.

Grant me a perfect end – your holy presence,

a blessed resurrection and life everlasting.

AMEN.

Teacher's Objectives

Appendix C

III. FRUITS OF THE HOLY SPIRIT

A. Charity
B. Joy
C. Peace
D. Patience

E. Kindness
F. Goodness
G. Longanimity
H. Mildness

I. Faith
J. Modesty
K. Continency
L. Chastity

Students should be able to:

1. Define the meaning of each of the twelve fruits of the Holy Spirit.
2. Know that these are gifts from God when we obey the Ten Commandments and live in God's love.
3. Know the fruits come from God's Spirit, the Holy Spirit, the third person of the Trinity. The Holy Spirit is all twelve named fruits and shares these attributes with us.
4. Know that these fruits grow in us the more we use them.
5. Know that these fruits can spread from person to person and attract others to God.

Background for the Teacher

ETHICS: "Peter Kreeft reminds us that 'ethics without virtue is illusion.' He is moved by the Christian perception that virtue is the fruit of faith," Russell Kirk says in the forward of *Back to Virtue*. But before we can understand and teach virtue, we need to grow in knowledge of virtue, which in our day is so often confused with vice. "However, to practice morality, we must first know it. To be men and women of virtue, not vice, we must know what virtue and vice mean," Kreeft states.

FRUITS: In *The Faith Explained*, Leo J. Trese asserts:

"The fruits of the Holy Spirit are just that: the outward fruits of the inner life, the external product of the indwelling of Spirit ... the twelve fruits are the broad brush strokes which outline for us the portrait of a truly Christian man – or woman ... What kind of person is it who lives habitually in the state of sanctifying grace, and who tries perserveringly (sic.) to subordinate self to the working of grace?

"First of all he is an unselfish person. He sees Christ in his neighbor and is considerate to others ... even at the cost of inconvenience and hardship to himself. This is charity.

"Then he is a cheerful and pleasant sort of person. He seems to radiate an inner glow, which makes itself felt in any group of which he is a part. When he is around, the sun seems to shine a little brighter ... This is joy.

"He is a quiet and relaxed person. Psychologists would call him well adjusted. His brow may be puckered with thought, but seldom with worry. He is a steady sort of person ... this is peace.

"He is not easily angered, he is not resentful of slights. He is not upset or frustrated when things go wrong ... He can fall six times and still start over the seventh time without grinding his teeth and cursing his luck. This is patience.

"Hs is a kind person. People come to him with their troubles, and find him a sympathetic listener; they go away feeling better just for having talked with him. He is interested in the enthusiasms and problems of others ... This is benignity (kindness).

"He stands solidly for what is right, even when it means standing alone. He is not self-righteous; he does not judge others; he is slow to criticize and still slower to condemn; he is forbearing with the ignorance and the weakness of others. But he will not compromise principle, he will not temporize with evil ... This is goodness.

"He is uncomplaining under pain and disappointment, in sickness and in sorrow. Self-pity is unknown to him. He will raise his tear-stained eyes to heaven in prayer but never in rebellion. This is long suffering (longanimity).

"He is a gentle person … He gives his best to whatever task comes to hand, but without any of the aggressiveness of the "go-getter." He does not seek to dominate others. He will reason persuasively, but he is never argumentative. This is mildness.

"He is proud of his membership in Christ's mystical body. He does not try to ram his religion down anyone's throat, but neither is he apologetic for what he believes. He does not try to conceal his religion in public; he is quick to defend the truth when it is attacked in his presence; his religion is the most important thing in life to him. This is faith.

"His love for Jesus Christ makes him recoil from the thought of being an ally of the devil, from the thought of occasioning sin to another. In dress and deportment and speech, there is a decency about him or her which fortifies rather than weakens others in their virtue. This is modesty.

"He is a temperate person, with his passions firmly ruled by reason and by grace. He is not up in the clouds today and down in the depths tomorrow. Whether it is in eating or in drinking, whether at work or at play, he manifests an admirable self-control in all he does. This is continency.

"He has a great reverence for the procreative power that God has given him, a holy awe that God should have so shared his creative power with humankind. He sees sex as something precious and sacred, a bond of union to be used only within the limits of wedlock and for the purpose established by God; never as a plaything, as a source of self-gratification. This is chastity."

Prayer: For A Magnanimous Heart

(Queen Mary Stuart, 1542-1587)

Keep us O God, from all pettiness.

Let us be large in thought, in word, in deed.

Let us be done with faultfinding

and leave off all self-seeking.

May we put away all pretense and meet each

other face to face,

without self-pity and without prejudice.

May we never be hasty in judgment,

and always be generous.

Let us take time for all things,

and make us grow calm, serene and gentle.

Teach us to put into action our better impulses,

to be straightforward and unafraid.

Grant that we may realize

that it is the little things of life that create differences,

that in the big things of life we are as one.

And, O Lord God, let us not forget to be kind!

Teacher's Objectives

Appendix D
IV. SEVEN CAPITAL SINS

A. Pride
B. Covetousness
C. Lust
D. Anger
E. Gluttony
F. Envy
G. Sloth

Students should be able to:

1. Define each of the seven capital sins.
2. List from memory the seven capital sins.
3. Know why the seven capital sins offend God.
4. Give positive examples of avoiding these sins.
5. Know that the theological virtue of hope will help them avoid these sins and will also lead them back to God through the Sacrament of Reconciliation if they should sin.

Background for the Teacher

Saint Pope John Paul II, in his address to the young people of Rome, December 20, 1978, said, "Sin! The catechism tells us that it is transgression of God's commandment. We know that by it the Lord is offended, friendship with him is broken, his grace is lost, one strays from the right path, heading for ruin ... Sin is to ignore, trample upon, transgress these wise and useful rules which the Lord gave us, that is why it is disorder and ruin! With so many "voices" inside and outside us, it tempts us, that is, urges us not to believe in God, not to listen to his Fatherly invitations, to prefer our whim to his friendship. Committing sin, we are far from God, against God, without God!" And on December 2, 1984 he asserted further: "Clearly, sin is a product of man's freedom ... Exclusion of God, rupture with God, disobedience to God: throughout the history of mankind, this has been and is, in various forms, sin.

Saint Thomas Aquinas points out: "Through sin, the soul commits a disorder that reaches the point of turning away from its ultimate end – God – to which it is bound by charity, then the sin is mortal; on the other hand, whenever the disorder does not reach the point of a turning away from God, the sin is venial."

Saint Pope John Paul II, on December 2, 1984, stated:

"It is not true that modern man is threatened by an eclipse of conscience? By a deformation of conscience? By a numbness of deadening of conscience? ... My predecessor Pius XII one day declared, in words that have almost become proverbial, that **'the sin of the century is the loss of the sense of sin' ... Secularism is by nature and definition a movement of ideas and behavior which advocates a humanism totally without God, completely centered upon the cult of action and production and caught up in the heady enthusiasm of consumerism and pleasure seeking, unconcerned with the danger of 'losing one's soul.'** This secularism cannot but undermine the sense of sin. At the very most, sin will be reduced to what offends man ... **It is therefore vain to hope that there will take root a sense of sin against man and against human values, if there is no sense of offense against God, namely the true sense of sin.**

"Another reason for the disappearance of the sense of sin in contemporary society is to be found in the errors made in evaluating certain findings of the human sciences. Thus on the basis of certain affirmations of psychology, concern to avoid certain feelings of guilt, or to place limits on freedom leads to a refusal ever to admit any shortcoming ... all failings are blamed upon society, and the individual is declared innocent of them.

"The sense of sin also easily declines as a result of a system of ethics deriving from a certain historical relativism. This may take the form of an ethical system which relativizes the moral norm, denying its absolute and unconditional value and as a consequence denying that there can be intrinsically illicit acts ... **An effect of this ethical turning upside down is always such an attenuation of**

the notion of sin as almost to reach the point of saying that sin does exist, but no one knows who commits it.

"Finally, **the sense of sin disappears, when it is wrongly identified with a morbid feeling of guilt, or with the mere transgression of legal norms and precepts …**

"Even in the field of thought and life of the Church certain trends inevitably favor the decline of the sense of sin. For example, **some are inclined to replace exaggerated attitudes of the past with other exaggerations: from too much emphasis on the fear of eternal punishment they pass to preaching a love of God that excludes any punishment deserved by sin; from severity in trying to correct erroneous conscience they pass to a kind of respect for conscience which excludes the duty of telling the truth."**

Prayer

(St. Thomas More, 1478-1535)

Lord, grant me a holy heart

that sees always what is fine and pure

and is not frightened at the sight of sin,

but creates order wherever it goes.

Grant me a heart that knows nothing

of boredom, weeping and sighing.

Let me not be too concerned

with the bothersome thing

I call "myself."

Prayer to St. Michael

St. Michael the Archangel

defend us in battle;

be our defense against the wickedness

and snares of the devil.

May God rebuke him, we humbly pray.

And to you, O Prince of the heavenly host,

by the power of God thrust into hell Satan

and all the evil spirits

who prowl about the world for the ruin of souls.

AMEN.

Teacher's Objectives

Appendix E

V. THE OPPOSITE VIRTUES (for sins of):

A.	Humility	(Pride)
B.	Generosity	(Covetousness)
C.	Chastity	(Lust)
D.	Meekness	(Anger)
E.	Temperance	(Gluttony)
F.	Brotherly Love	(Envy)
G.	Diligence	(Sloth)

Students should be able to:

1. Define the seven opposite virtues.
2. Know which opposite virtue is the alternative to its corresponding capital sin.
3. Know that these virtues are our free choices. We are never forced to sin.
4. Know that these virtues will grow the more they are practiced.
5. Give examples of practicing these virtues at home, at school, and with their friends, families and neighbors.

Background for the Teacher

"Jesus ... gives us the road map for our lives," Peter Kreeft says in *Back to Virtue*. Pointing to the Beatitudes, he writes:

"This is the greatest of all treasure maps to the greatest of all treasures, and it is given to us absolutely free ... the double-edged character of the Beatitudes is clear ... that seven of the nine Beatitudes are the opposites to the seven deadly sins. The poor in spirit, who are detached from riches, are the opposite the avaricious, who are addicted to them. Those who mourn, who are empty of pleasure, are the opposite of the gluttonous, who are filled with pleasures. The meek are the opposite of the proud. Those who hunger and thirst for righteousness are the opposite of the slothful, who lack spiritual ambition. The pure of heart are the opposite of the lustful. The peacemakers are the opposite of the wrathful. And those who are persecuted for righteousness' sake, that is, those who are willing to suffer for good, are the opposite of the envious, who are unwilling to have less satisfaction or more suffering than others."

THE BEATITUDES

(Matthew 5:3-12)

Blessed are the poor in spirit, the kingdom of heaven is theirs.

Blessed are those who mourn, for they shall be comforted.

Blessed are the meek, for they shall inherit the earth.

Blessed are those who hunger and thirst for righteousness, for they shall be satisfied.

Blessed are the merciful, for they shall obtain mercy.

Blessed are the pure in heart, for they shall see God.

Blessed the peacemakers, for they shall be called sons of God.

Blessed are those who are persecuted for righteousness' sake, for theirs is the kingdom of heaven.

Blessed are you when men revile you and persecute you and utter all kinds of evil against you falsely on my account. Rejoice and be glad, for your reward is great in heaven, for so men persecuted the prophets who were before you."

A Prayer For Peacemakers

(Pope Paul VI, 1897-1978)

O Lord, God of peace, you have created us and shown us your love so that we may share in your glory. We bless you and give thanks because you have sent us Jesus, your well-beloved Son. Through the mystery of his resurrection, you made him the worker of salvation, the source of peace, the bond of brotherhood. We give thanks for the desires, efforts and achievements stirred up by the Spirit of peace in our time, to replace hate by love, mistrust by understanding, indifference by interdependence. Open our minds and hearts to the real demands of love, so that we may all become more completely peacemakers. Remember, Father of mercy, all who struggle, suffer and idle to bring forth a world of closer relationship. May your kingdom of justice, peace and love come to people of every race and tongue. May the earth be filled with your glory.

Teacher's Objectives

Appendix F

VI. FRIENDSHIP

A. Characteristics
B. Mutual Respect
C. Expectations
D. Sincerity
E. Loyalty

F. Faithfulness
G. Honesty
H. Purity
I. Self-Esteem

Students should be able to:

1. Know that friendship arises out of virtue. Where there is no virtue, there is no friendship.
2. Name at least five characteristics (virtues) of friendship: sincerity, loyalty, faithfulness, honesty and purity.
3. Know that friends have mutual respect for each other.
4. Know that friends do not speak, dress, or coax in ways that rob their friend's self-esteem.
5. Define the five virtues of friendship mentioned above and explain how these virtues relate to their own friends (in a positive way).

Background for the Teacher

Jesus tells us in Matthew 22:39: "You shall love your neighbor as yourself."

"This commandment of the Lord must be your inspiration in forming true human relationships among yourselves, so that nobody will ever feel alone or unwanted, or much less, rejected, despised or hated," Saint Pope John Paul II said on October3, 1979, at Shea Stadium. "To love is, therefore, essentially to give oneself to others … To be able to love truly. It is necessary to detach oneself from many things and above all from oneself – a long and demanding task … is exhausting and exalting … It is the secret of happiness," Saint Pope John Paull II said to the young people of France in June 1980.

Dr. David Isaacs writes in *Character Building*:

"Friendship presupposes a certain togetherness, a meeting of minds and feelings and desires ... If there is respect, flexibility and a real desire on the part of both to help each other, to find the truth, then a deep friendship can develop ... A good friend makes (wholesome) demands on his friend, is understanding with him, is an example to him, gives him what he needs – neither more nor less – and finds time to spend with him. Nowadays we are very mean with the time we devote to friends and that makes no sense; it is inhuman ... friendship means a very close relationship. Therefore, a person cannot have a deep friendship until he has reached the point of discovering his own intimacy and of learning how to share it with others. In this sense, it is useful to distinguish friendship from other acts related to it. 'Sociability extends to everyone; love to one's neighbor, to the people about; friendship to one's intimates.' But in real life, it is difficult for friendships to arise unless one gets involved with people in general. It is a question of having lots of social relationships and practicing the Christian virtue of charity with everyone, because only in that way can mutual sympathy and rapport arise and friendship develop."

Prayer: Act of Charity

O my God, I love You above all things,

with my whole heart and soul,

because You are all good and worthy of all my love.

I love my neighbor as myself for the love of You.

I forgive all who have injured me,

and ask pardon of all whom I have injured.

AMEN.

Teacher's Objectives

Appendix G

VII. DECISION MAKING

A. Free Will
B. Coercion
C. Responsibility
D. Exploitation
E. Peer Pressure
F. Character

Students should be able to:

1. Define strength of character, God's gift of freedom in free will, coercion, exploitation, human respect (people's opinions), and responsibility.
2. Know that we are responsible for our own decisions and actions.
3. Know that it is only by giving someone else our permission, giving in, that coercion or exploitation is successful.
4. Know that we need to make decisions based on our family and Church teaching, not based on human respect of what other people think, not based in negative peer pressure.
5. Know that God will never force, or coerce us to love or follow Him, that God respects the freedom He gave us to choose freely to live by the Ten Commandments, and that God is always there for us to turn to, to guide us, to forgive us, to love us.

Background for Teacher

In a message to students on August 30, 1980, Saint Pope John Paul II said:

"Be consistent! Christian faith, our own dignity and the expectation of the present-day world, essentially need this commitment of consistency. And the first fundamental expression of consistency is the struggle against sin, that is, the constant and even heroic effort to live in grace. Unfortunately we live in an age in which sin has even become an industry, which produces money, inspires economic plans, bestows prosperity. This situation is certainly striking and terrible. Yet we must not let ourselves be frightened or oppressed; any age demands 'consistency' from the Christian.

"And so, even in present-day society, immersed in a lay and permissive atmosphere, which may tempt and entice, you young people remain consistent with the message and friendship of Jesus; live in grace, abide in his love, putting into practice the whole moral law, nourishing your soul with the Body of Christ, taking advantage of the Sacrament of Penance periodically and seriously ... You, too, be courageous! The world needs convinced and fearless witnesses. It is not enough to discuss, it is necessary to act! Let your consistency become witness and let the first form of this commitment be 'availability.' Always feel ready, like the Good Samaritan, to love, to assist, to help, in the family, at work, in recreation, with those who are near and those who are far away."

In regard to decisions, Saint Pope John Paul II, when speaking to the youth of Apulia, Italy on October 5, 1980, said:

"All decision making needs a solid base from which to draw, a wellspring, a data base with honest input, consistent with the department upon the truths of our faith. The Christian must always be consistent with his faith. 'Martyrdom,' Clemente Alessandrino wrote, 'consists in bearing witness to God. But every soul that seeks knowledge of God with purity, obeys God's commandments, is a martyr, both in life and in words. For if it does not shed its blood, it pours out its faith, since, for faith it separates from the body and even before dying' (Stromata) ... My great Predecessor Paul V, on October 30, 1968, after speaking on the authenticity of faith, O young people, may be certain, that is, founded on the Word of God, on deep knowledge of the Gospel message, and especially of the life, person and work of Christ; and also on the interior witness of the Holy Spirit. May your faith be strong; may it not hesitate, nor waiver, before the doubts, the uncertainties which philosophical systems or fashionable movements would like to suggest too you; may it not descend to compromises with certain concepts, which would like

64

to present Christianity as a mere ideology of historical character, and therefore to be placed at the same level as so many others, not outdated. May your faith be joyful, because it is based on the awareness of possessing a divine gift ... Let your faith be active ..."

Prayer: Morning Offering

O Jesus, through the immaculate Heart of Mary, I offer you my prayers, works, joys and sufferings of this day for all the intentions of your Sacred Heart, in union with the Holy Sacrifice of the Mass throughout the world, in reparation for my sins, for the intentions of all my relatives and friends and in particular for the intentions of the Holy Father.

AMEN

Printed in the United States
By Bookmasters